Ridgefield Fights the Civil War

Ridgefield Fights the Civil War

BY
Charles Pankenier

WORTHY SHORTS™
NEW YORK

CIVIL WAR
A Worthy Shorts Monograph

Ridgefield Fights the Civil War
Copyright © 2011 by Charles Pankenier
(Revised, August, 2012)

Design and organizing elements © copyright 2011
by Worthy Shorts.

Sale of this work in this imprint or design, except by Worthy
Shorts or its agents, is prohibited.

Published by Worthy Shorts
The Online Private Press for Professionals

ISBN 978-1-935340-75-1
WS 158

Worthy Shorts® is a Registered Trademark.

Manufactured in the United States of America, or in Great Britain,
when purchased outside of the United States.

For more information, visit
www.WorthyShorts.com

Line of March

Foreword	vii
Acknowledgments	ix
Antebellum	1
The Irrepressible Conflict	3
The Election of 1860	6
War!	7
We Are Coming, Father Abra'am	10
A View From the Inn	13
Tenting Tonight	15
Seeing the Elephant	20
Gettysburg	23
From These Honored Dead	26
About Used Up	31
Trial and Decision	32
Florida Sojourn	34
Victory and Mourning	35
Epilogue	36
Notes	39
Principal Sources	43
Illustration Credits	44
Learning About Your Ridgefield Civil War Ancestor	45

Foreword

This brief narrative is not intended to be a complete and comprehensive treatment of the title subject. Rather, it draws from primary and secondary sources to recount the histories of particular individuals, organizations, and events to represent how Ridgefield, Connecticut soldiers and their loved ones on the home front experienced the desperate 1861-65 struggle that defined our country.

Acknowledgments

I wish to express my appreciation for the assistance of the following people: Kay Ables, Ridgefield Town Historian, past President of the Ridgefield Historical Society and keeper of the flame; Dirk Bollenback, distinguished former teacher at Ridgefield High School and historian of St. Stephen's Episcopal Church; Dale E. Call, dedicated creator and webmaster of the 17th Connecticut Volunteer Infantry website; George Hancock, knowledgeable student of *A View From the Inn* and generous member of the Keeler Tavern Museum; Jack Sanders, creator of *RidgefieldHistory.com*, an indispensable resource for understanding the story of the town and its people; and the staff members of the Ridgefield Library, who displayed endless patience in accommodating my sometimes quixotic requests.

I am grateful for their essential contributions, which are present throughout this history. The opinions and any errors herein are entirely the author's.

Charles Pankenier
January 2011

Antebellum

By 1860, Ridgefield, Connecticut had been settled for more than 150 years, a religious, political, and market center for the surrounding farms. In the decades of recovery following the Revolutionary War, subsistence agriculture was augmented by production of cash crops, often in the form of livestock products. As soon as the early 19th century, for example, Ridgefield exported 1,500 barrels each of beef and pork as well as nearly 17,000 pounds of butter each year, much of it likely headed to rapidly-growing New York City.

Although not graced with the same abundant water power as other Connecticut communities, Ridgefield nonetheless also had diversified mills and commercial activities that contributed to the town's self-sufficiency, some of them commemorated in the names of local roadways (Saw Mill Hill, Fulling Mill, Tannery Hill).

Shoemaking was a long-established activity in the town; by the 1850 Census, 100 or so men claimed it as an occupation.[1] As the Industrial Revolution transformed New England in the early 19th century, commercial activity in Ridgefield expanded to also include the manufacture of candlesticks and small metal implements; the only foundry between New Haven and the Hudson Valley; cabinet- and furniture-making (with mahogany and cherry items especially popular in the South); shirt-making; and the building of carriages in a facility known as the "Big Shop", located on land currently occupied by the Congregational Church at the corner of Main Street and West Lane. As with Ridgefield-made furniture, and somewhat ironically in light of future events, wealthy southerners were an important market, and the carriage firm—one of nearly 100 in the state—enjoyed sufficient business to maintain a sales office and showroom in New Orleans.

The town was well-served by the New England's rapidly-developing communications and transportation network. By 1852, railroad lines ran nearby from Norwalk to Danbury and through Brewster along New York's Harlem Valley line. There was also regular horse-drawn coach service from Norwalk, as well as from Philadelphia to New York City, Ridgefield, and on to Boston.

In the early 19th century, the taproom of William Keeler's Hotel brought townspeople and travelers together to discuss events of the day.

Passengers, together with agricultural and commercial products, could readily travel over the roads or be transported by rail and Long Island Sound steamboat to their destinations or for trans-shipment. Although Ridgefield did not have a telegraph office until 1866, coaches (and horsemen) brought not only a stream of informed visitors to town, but also the mail and a steady supply of newspapers and periodicals with reports and commentary on events of the day.

Population in this bustling and prosperous community remained stable from 1820 (when Ridgefield's 2,299 citizens were very likely outnumbered by the town's sheep) to 1860, when the count had declined slightly to 2,213 people, largely as a result of a steady outflow of migrants seeking farmland and futures to the west.

The Irrepressible Conflict

Through the first half of the 19th century, the United States experienced a growing division between North and South. While the sharpest conflict concerned slavery, the two sections increasingly diverged economically, politically, sociologically, and culturally. To generalize, the South remained largely rural, agrarian, and economically and socially static. The North, on the other hand, was increasingly urban and industrial, with greater economic and social dynamism in a much larger population. (Of the country's ten largest cities in 1860, only one—New Orleans—was located in the South; New York State, by itself, manufactured four times the goods of all the southern states).

During the 1850's, the country's political leaders attempted to deal with the growing sectional differences over slavery through legislative compromise. Their efforts, however, were often overtaken by events, many of them violent, which further polarized the body politic. The Fugitive Slave Act, one of the immediate byproducts of the Compromise of 1850, was openly opposed by northern legislatures, which made it a crime to obey federal law. Connecticut State Historian Albert Van Dusen wrote that the act "helped to create deeper antislavery feeling in Connecticut and the North generally than had ever existed previously," although the state had not actually outlawed slavery until 1848.

The act also spurred the operation of the Underground Railroad to spirit escaped slaves to freedom, with "safe houses" throughout the state, while Farmington served as "Grand Central Station", in the words of one historian. (By 1860, the number of African-Americans in Ridgefield had dwindled from nearly 30

Phillis Dubois, a free black woman, was virtually a member of Ridgefield's Resseguie family.

to eight; one was Phillis Dubois, a virtual member of the Resseguie family who participated with them in operating what we know now as the Keeler Tavern Museum and is buried with them in the family plot).

The 1852 publication of *Uncle Tom's Cabin* caused a sensation; it quickly sold a remarkable 300,000 copies and further incited passions on both sides of the slavery question. Resseguie daughter Anna Marie quickly obtained a copy and responded to the novel's humanity and pathos as she read it aloud to an attentive circle of friends.

Later, the Kansas-Nebraska Act led to guerilla warfare over slavery in "Bleeding Kansas". Abolitionist John Brown, born in northwest Connecticut, led a murderous anti-slavery rampage that was perhaps the most savage incident.

In 1853, a small gathering in Ripon, Wisconsin had conceived the Republican Party, dedicated to opposing further expansion of slavery into the territories. Three years later, the presidential campaign was emotional and bitterly fought, made more so by the vicious beating of a Massachusetts senator by a South Carolina congressman on the Senate floor. The 1856 election had a remarkable 83 percent turnout. Despite an election-eve torchlight parade by Ridgefield supporters of national Democratic winner James Buchanan, Republican presidential candidate John Charles Fremont carried Ridgefield by a 100-vote plurality, reflecting the town's prevailing anti-slavery sentiment.

As the decade drew to a close, the Dred Scott decision of 1857 and John Brown's 1859 raid at Harper's Ferry were used by partisans on both sides to further inflame emotions already rubbed raw.

The Election of 1860

The presidential election year of 1860 brought the country's long-festering political crisis to a head. In March, Ridgefield's newly-completed Catoonah Hall—which stood on its namesake street—attracted a reported crowd of 600 people to hear Charles Case, an Indiana congressman, speak against slavery and in favor of the Republican Party. The principal plank of the Republican platform, as in 1856, opposed expansion of slavery, although candidate Abraham Lincoln's statements during the campaign were few and carefully hedged. The opposition was divided among three men, two of them representing largely sectional interests, with the remaining faction more concerned about the threat of disunion than the morality of slavery. As a result, although Lincoln captured less than 40 percent of the popular vote (in part because he did not even appear on the ballot in ten southern states), he achieved a substantial majority of electoral votes, carrying every county in New England, for example. Torchlight parades by young Republicans called "Wide Awakes" (one October evening saw between 300 and 400 people marching back and forth on Ridgefield's Main Street) presaged the 1860 election results in town, which were even more decisive than for Connecticut as a whole:

	Ridgefield	Connecticut
Lincoln	291 (66%)	43,488 (58%)
Douglas	3	15,431
Breckinridge	114	14,392
Others	30	1,528

As with nature, politics abhors a vacuum and, with over four months between Lincoln's November election and his March 1861 inauguration, disaffected southern states moved to fill it. Led by South Carolina in December, a total of seven states voted to secede from the union before Lincoln could take office.

War!

By February, 1861 the seceding states had formed a Confederate government with Jefferson Davis at its head. Those states claimed possession of federal forts, armories, and other property within their boundaries, a claim disputed by the U.S. government, which asserted that there was no legal basis for secession.

Fort Sumter, a key facility dominating the harbor at Charleston, S.C., became a flashpoint in April when Confederate forces demanded its surrender before it could be re-supplied. The federal commander refused, and surrounding Rebel batteries opened fire on April 12; the handful of U.S. troops was forced to evacuate after a 34-hour bombardment.

The encounter electrified North and South; secession was longer merely a political abstraction, but an act of war. In immediate response, Lincoln called on the states to provide 75,000 troops to serve for 90 days to put down the insurrection and re-occupy federal property; four more southern states seceded rather than take up arms against their neighbors.

In a journal of her life from 1851-67, Anna Marie Resseguie recorded the *"startling news"* of Sumter's surrender and, a few days later, the virtual celebration in Ridgefield, as bands played, a cannon was fired,

Today's landmark Keeler Tavern Museum was the Resseguie Hotel, home and family business as Anna Marie kept the journal that records life on the Ridgefield home front during the war years.

and flags were raised in front of homes. Within hours of Lincoln's call, two Ridgefield men rushed to join Danbury's Wooster Guards, a local militia named for the Revolutionary War general slain in the Battle of Ridgefield. The community's somewhat giddy response was not unusual. Pulitzer Prize-winning Civil War historian Bruce Catton observed that "An unsophisticated people surged out under waving flags with glad cries and laughter, as if the thing that had happened called for rejoicing."

Ridgefield came by its naivete honestly. While Selectman Ebenezer Hawley was one of several village veterans of the War of 1812 (most with service records shorter than 60 days), and there were at least two residents who had served during the conflict with

Mexico, it is likely that no more than a dozen living citizens had any experience of the active military, much less of the battlefield. For Ridgefield volunteers, as for thousands elsewhere who stepped forward, a 90-day enlistment appeared to be an opportunity for a brief, glorious adventure in a noble cause.

The patriotic fervor took both symbolic and practical forms. A town meeting on May 4 swore "the oath of fidelity to the sacred flag of our country..." More tangibly, Ridgefield voted a stipend of $2 per week to the wife of each man who volunteered, with 50 cents to be paid for each child under 12.

North and South, the forces gathered through the spring. Goaded by popular pressure and northern newspapers to move "On to Richmond!", the Confederate capital, the untrained federal army marched from its Washington camps into northern Virginia in late July to confront the Rebel forces near a stream called Bull Run. The troops were accompanied by throngs of civilian picnickers, including Connecticut Senator Lafayette Foster, eager to witness the certain federal triumph as a kind of holiday entertainment.

The ensuing Union defeat and disorderly retreat, with the 4,700 casualties on both sides widely reported as the greatest in the history of the North American continent, were shocking. They shattered many illusions in the North, and introduced a sobering reality: putting down the insurrection was likely to be a bloody and protracted affair.

Anna Marie's July 24, 1861 diary entry reflects a cool and dispassionate appraisal of the battle, its consequences, and its effect on Union morale. *"Instead of being dispirited, the North is more determined than ever..."*

she wrote, accurately capturing the mood of the country. That resolve would be sorely tested in the years to come, and it was hardly universal: Historian Van Dusen noted that "at Ridgefield a man who expressed satisfaction over the Bull Run disaster was thoroughly ducked under the town pump".

Meanwhile, village women gathered at the home of Mrs. William Seymour to sew hospital garments for soldiers.

We Are Coming, Father Abra'am

Through the first twelve months that the armies contended, 50 Ridgefield men volunteered for military service, as the Lincoln administration issued repeated calls for troops, eventually for three-year terms. By war's end, some 200 Ridgefield people would serve in the conflict, including one who soldiered for the Confederacy.

(Some perspective: the roughly 200 represented approximately 40 percent of the number capable of military service in the community. The available manpower pool of about 500 men is reckoned by subtracting from the town's 1,100 males those too young, too old, and immediately disqualified on account of physical infirmity. A principal infirmity was a fairly common affliction—the absence of teeth, essential for tearing open the paper cartridges that held Civil War ammunition.)

If the Ridgefield soldiers were typical of their average Union comrades-in-arms, they were around age 25, stood about 5 feet 8 inches tall, and weighed 143 pounds. Despite the growth of commercial and industrial activity, approximately half of the Union army came from rural, agricultural backgrounds.

The men joined and served in regiments, organized by states; by 1862, regiments often were composed of men from the same locality. Three Ridgefield men named Austin, for example, enlisted in the same regiment on the same August day in that year; David, Hiram, and Jacob all were assigned to the same company.

The regiment was the fundamental building block of both armies. Initially comprising approximately 1,000 men organized in ten companies, it was how soldiers were recruited, were trained and supplied, marched, camped, and were deployed in battle. In many respects, the regiment became a surrogate for the small communities many of the men had left behind, so it is not surprising that, after the war, the regiment was the focal point around which histories were written, reunions were held, and monuments were erected on former battlefields.

The "local" character of the regimental organization had notable advantages—and disadvantages. To begin with, the presence of friends and neighbors—even relatives—eased the transition to the rigors of military life for young men far from home for the first time; in the event of wound or illness, there were familiar faces to provide care and support. In military terms, that same familiarity promoted what is now called "unit cohesion" in the ranks and, most important, in battle: no one wished to display cowardice and be judged a pariah among his neighbors in the community.

At the same time, a single battle could inflict devastating losses on a small community or even a single family. Moreover, unit cohesion had a double edge; if a formal or informal leader lost his nerve, that provided sanction for others to do likewise. Like him, they could

Ridgefield recruit Phineas Lounsbury. He later served as Connecticut governor and built the stately home now used as the Community Center.

break and run, and a charge or defensive position could dissolve in an instant.

Ridgefield natives enlisted in at least 20 different Connecticut regiments as well as those from other states, chiefly New York. The greatest response came in an eight-week period from July to September 1862, when more than 85 men rallied to the colors for three years' service, some returning from afar to enlist in their hometown.

They were motivated by patriotism, no doubt, but also perhaps by the threat of a draft if Ridgefield did not meet its assigned quota for volunteers, and particularly by the town's August 9 establishment of a $200 bounty for each man who joined a Connecticut regiment by August 20 (later extended), in addition to the $100 federal recruitment bonus. It can hardly be a coincidence that

75 men enlisted within the next month, a remarkable 19 just two days later on August 11 alone (including future Connecticut governor Phineas Lounsbury), with another 17 signing up on August 13.

(A precise figure for median income in Ridgefield in 1862 is not easy to establish. The minister of the Congregational church, a leading professional, earned approximately $700 per year, supplemented by contributions from parishioners. A reasonable estimate for the typical workingman is about $400 annually, with the median affected by the generally lower cash wages paid to agricultural workers. A total cash enlistment bonus of $300, therefore, represented well over six months' income for many men, especially attractive in light of a Union private's pay of $13 per month. Ridgefield's outlay for bonuses for late summer volunteers would have totaled almost $16,000—likely as much or more than annual community spending for schools, roads and other expenses).

The overwhelming majority was assigned to Company G of the 17th Connecticut Volunteer Infantry(CVI), with another dozen or so joining Company C to form by far the greatest concentration of Ridgefield soldiers within a single unit. This newly-created "Fairfield County Regiment" was the state's first "local" regiment of the war.

A View From the Inn

Anna Marie's journal of Ridgefield during the war years is a record of the resolutely day-to-day and personal (visits by relatives and friends, names of guests at the inn, trips and outings, illnesses, sermon topics) juxtaposed with keenly-judged notations about some of the war's significant military and political developments—the 1861 appointment of the young and dashing George McClellan to lead the main Union army in the East, federal successes in the West and Carolinas during early 1862, the standoff between the Monitor and Merrimac, the appalling casualties at the Battle of Shiloh, the capture of New Orleans in April 1862. (It is interesting to speculate on whether the very few Ridgefield natives in the Connecticut 9th and 12th regiments, part of the force that occupied New Orleans, had occasion to march past the former showroom and offices of their hometown carriage company).

While it is unfair to expect Anna Marie to have been a one-woman Ridgefield Press (the newspaper was not published until 1875), her journal has less room for community events, making her expression of feeling surrounding the *"strange sad spectacle"* of the August 16, 1862 Ridgefield recruits' departure march all the more notable, especially since it is accompanied by her observation that *"All feel that the prospects for our country are very gloomy, and good men believe that many more thousands of lives must be sacrificed…"*

Anna Marie had proven herself a reliable reporter and perceptive commentator on major military events, so her journal during the summer of 1862 is noteworthy for its uncharacteristic omissions, including any mention of the unhappy outcome of the largest and most ambitious Union military effort of the war--one that merited an unusual front-page article in the *Danbury Times*: General McClellan's massive spring 1862 offensive aimed at capturing the Confederate capital of Richmond and ending the conflict in the East. The campaign culminated in a series of battles called the Seven Days, once again with unprecedented casualties, and ended with McClellan's repulse by Robert E. Lee, followed by humiliating withdrawal. Nor, after the recruits had marched off in August, is there any reference in the diary to the bloody federal debacle at Second Bull Run days later. From Anna Marie's somber outlook, it appears that Ridgefield residents were being borne down by the defeats in the Eastern Theater and by the rapidly-growing casualty lists among relatives and neighbors after more than a year of war.

Tenting Tonight

The Ridgefield volunteers who set off for what is now Bridgeport's Seaside Park in summer 1862 joined men from other Fairfield County towns for an August 28 mustering-in as members of the Connecticut 17th Volunteer Infantry, eventually to become part of the XI Corps of the Army of the Potomac.

During the course of the Civil War, a cumulative total of more than 2 million men served in the federal forces. By contrast, in 1861 the Union could call on fewer than 800 active-duty West Point graduates to serve as officers, some of whom—the flamboyant George Armstrong Custer, for example—had inevitably finished at, or near, the bottom of their classes (although Custer later became the youngest general in American military history).

Because trained military officers were in such short supply, tens of thousands of civilians were required to learn on the job at every level. The colonels who led individual

The Seventeenth Connecticut Volunteer Infantry

The greatest number of Ridgefield men were enrolled in Companies C and G of the 17th Connecticut Volunteer Infantry, the "Fairfield County" regiment

regiments were often appointed by the state's governor, who could use the position to reward the politically powerful, or his supporters, friends, and family members, as well as to sideline potential political opponents. Some men proved to be adept military officers and were remarkably successful (fully one-third of Union generals had no pre-war military experience; at least some of them deserved promotion on merit). A much larger number occupied a vast middle ground where they displayed widely varying degrees of competence; and, regrettably, a sizeable number were disasters—dim-witted, or chronic drunkards, or cowardly. For many soldiers, the quality of the man who served as their regimental commander was a matter of luck and happenstance.

The colonel of the Connecticut 17th was William Noble of Bridgeport, a businessman who partnered with none other than P. T. Barnum in the development of East Bridgeport, where he created the Park City's first park, and where many of the streets are named for members of the Noble family. The colonel led his men through crowds of family and friends as they departed Bridgeport for the front on September 3 and arrived in camp around Baltimore shortly thereafter. (As the regiment was

Colonel William Noble, Bridgeport business partner of P. T. Barnum, was appointed commander of the 17th CVI.

settling in, the first Ridgefield soldier of the war was killed 235 miles to the north, when Joseph Hawkins, home on furlough from the 14th New York, was hit by a cannon during a celebration in Norwalk. Corporal Henry Keeler, the first Ridgefielder to perish in combat, fell mortally wounded days later in western Maryland[2]).

Absent a trove of letters from Ridgefield soldiers describing the specifics of their military lives, we are limited to informed speculation drawn from the testimony of their comrades-in-arms.

For example, how a regiment was trained was largely at the discretion of individual regimental commanders. While Colonel Noble did not record his approach, it likely involved endless hours of drill—essentially, practice in moving and maneuvering a large body of untrained officers and recruits, especially in how to deploy from a marching column of two or four abreast into a front several hundred yards wide, and how to shift the axis of that front as required by developments in battle.

Aside from marching drills, there was little or no physical training. Men were expected to be able to travel 16 to 20 miles a day while carrying 30 pounds or more, including a weapon, a blanket roll, poncho, and tent half, personal items, a haversack (a canvas bag containing cooked rations), a canteen, and possibly a coffee pot or frying pan.

It is probable that the weapon carried by at least some Ridgefield men was the Enfield rifle-musket, a British-made shoulder arm widely used by both sides. It was a 9 1/2-pound, percussion-fired, muzzle-loaded weapon; an experienced infantryman could manage as many as three shots per minute. Although men drilled repeatedly in the at least 10 separate actions required to load and shoot, it was not unusual for a recruit to enter his first battle having fired no more than a dozen practice rounds. Nonetheless, the rifle-musket was an immensely destructive weapon. Its superior range, combined with its ballistic impact, rendered existing offensive infantry doctrine largely obsolete, as technology outstripped tactics.

For most men, camp was also a first-time experience in communal living, with shared cooking fires, sleeping quarters, and latrines, or "sinks". These close quarters exacted a high price especially among the farm boys, whose immune systems were the most susceptible to the measles, chicken pox, and mumps that raged through the camps, although typhoid, dysentery, and pneumonia were the truly devastating killers.

Sanitation, hygiene, and medical care all were primitive; by war's end, nearly 200,000 Union soldiers had died of disease, almost double the toll from battlefield deaths and wounds, awful as that carnage was.

Nor did the troops' diet contribute much to health. While camp food might include some fresh vegetables and fruits, much of the menu on the march consisted of a high-calorie cracker called hardtack, fatty bacon or salt pork, and coffee. Newly-baked hardtack was reasonably tasty and satisfying, but as the crackers aged they could become what soldiers called "worm castles", home to weevils. Stale hardtack often required crumbling with a rifle butt or soaking in coffee or bacon grease to render it edible. (For a discussion of a canned Civil War "energy drink" with a local connection, see the "History of Borden's Condensed Milk").

There is little independent evaluation of Colonel Noble's executive and military abilities. On one hand, he was willing to incur the wrath of the local commanding general and appeal to the War Department when he believed his men were being ill-treated in the Baltimore camp. As a result, the regiment was abruptly and angrily ordered to relocate. On the other hand, in early 1863 Noble was the object of an abortive "mutiny" by his subordinate officers, which collapsed when they ultimately confessed their "wrongdoing". Following the war, Noble's lucrative career pursuing pensions for Union veterans was briefly disrupted by an arrest for fraud, for which he paid a fine. It appears that the colonel was one of those officers who occupied that vast middle ground of competency—and of human frailty.

Because of accidents of timing, training, and assignment, the Connecticut 17th avoided two of the

Army of the Potomac's bloodiest encounters in the fall of 1862: Antietam in Maryland, and Fredricksburg, Virginia. In some respects, that escape would be the last bit of good luck the regiment would experience.

Seeing the Elephant

First came the infamous "Mud March".

Eager to redeem his reputation and to restore morale in the Army of the Potomac following his December humiliation at Fredricksburg, commanding general Ambrose Burnside launched a daring January 1863 attempt to out-maneuver and surprise Robert E. Lee. Unfortunately, the heavens opened over northern Virginia and the army, including the Connecticut 17th, bogged down in a quagmire, with wagons buried hub-deep, cannons sunk to their barrels, and men to their knees. The effort collapsed after two strenuous, fruitless, and tragicomic days in the mud. The army returned to winter camp, and Burnside was relieved of command shortly thereafter.

As they waited for the drying of the roads in April, the soldiers of the Connecticut 17th were seven months into their service and had yet to "see the elephant", the term used by Civil War soldiers to describe actual combat experience. (The phrase was common at least as early as the gold rushers of 1849, who appropriated the term from veterans of the Mexican War and used it as a metaphor to describe the remarkable and exotic sights they encountered as they crossed the continent.)

The regiment was about to make the elephant's acquaintance. New army commanding general Joseph

O. O. Howard, newly-elevated to command of XI Corps, including the 17th Connecticut, before the Battle of Chancellorsville.

Hooker—the third in less than six months—had his staff conceive a strategically impeccable plan for a spring offensive; unfortunately, Hooker appears to have developed a want of nerve as he actually executed it. As a result, by May 1 the Union army was aligned in an essentially defensive position near a one-house northern Virginia hamlet named Chancellorsville, with the XI Corps, including the Connecticut 17th, posted on the extreme right flank.

That exposed position, together with inept leadership and unfortunate circumstance, would combine to make the first sight of the elephant a disastrous one. To begin with, XI Corps was commanded by O.O. Howard, a newly-elevated general who left his troops largely unprepared to defend their position. Moreover, the corps was heavily populated by German immigrants, whose immigrant insularity and unfamiliarity with American military culture combined with nativist prejudice to produce a somewhat checkered history and reputation. Finally, the 17th was part of the nearly one-third of the corps with no prior combat experience.

In one of the most audacious tactical gambles—and achievements—in the history of warfare, Robert E. Lee violated a fundamental military principle by dividing his army in the face of a vastly superior enemy. He dispatched Stonewall Jackson and a force of as many as 28,000 Confederates on a rapid, screened march across the Union front, with the objective of "crossing the T"—getting beyond and then falling on the federal right flank with surprise and overwhelming numbers, rolling up the Union line like a runaway window shade. Manning that flank, of course, were the soldiers of the XI Corps, including the Connecticut 17th.

In fact, some of the Ridgefield men of Company G were probably deployed as pickets, a kind of human trip wire posted beyond the main line. Amid the growing sound of gunfire, they came tumbling back, accompanied by frightened deer, rabbits, and other animals pouring out of the brush. Soon there was heard the chilling Rebel yell, as Confederates burst from the woods and onto the surprised Yankees, many busy playing cards or cooking dinner.

The result was, in short, one of the greatest disasters ever to befall the U.S. military. Nearly two miles of the federal line ultimately dissolved in the face of the onrushing Confederates. By all accounts, the still-raw recruits of the 17th Connecticut acquitted themselves well in their baptism of fire during the debacle, resisting longer and in a more disciplined way than many of their colleagues. They drew approving mention from notable northern editor Horace Greeley, who singled out their performance during the assault, which lost momentum only on account of darkness and the propensity of Confederate enlisted men for halting to enjoy federal dinners left cooking over campfires, or ransacking abandoned tents for valuables.

A Union defensive line was eventually re-established and the 17th Connecticut re-grouped. Casualties in the unit of slightly more than 500 men totaled 120 killed, wounded, and missing, including Colonel Noble, who was wounded and out of action for the next two months. Four Ridgefield soldiers from Company C and six from Company G—already reduced by some 35 men (Phineas Lounsbury among them) on account of seven months of camp deaths and disability discharges—were wounded, captured, or both.

Gettysburg

Convinced of the near-invincibility of his troops, determined to relieve the war-torn counties of northern Virginia, and intent on demonstrating that further Union pursuit of the war was fruitless, Robert E. Lee launched his second invasion of the North and put his soldiers on the march in June 1863.

As units of Lee's army reached scattered locations in south-central Pennsylvania, they were screened from Washington, D.C by the Army of the Potomac, which moved in parallel as a blocking force. Concerned that his army might be destroyed piecemeal, Lee ordered its elements to concentrate on a small town called

Gettysburg. It was there, over the course of three days, that the most iconic and the bloodiest battle of the Civil War took place.

Lee's gathering forces were confronted by the units of the federal army northwest of the small town on the morning of July 1. As the 17th Connecticut double-quicked along the muddy roads toward the encounter, morale could not have been good. After the Chancellorsville rout, the XI Corps had been scapegoated by fellow Union soldiers, derided as "Howard's Cowards" or the "Flying Dutchmen", and they could not have had great confidence in their leadership.

The 17th arrived on the field around 3 p.m., in time to be moved forward by a young, ambitious, and aggressive new division commander. Six companies were directed to occupy what came to be known, after him, as "Barlow's Knoll". Eerily reminiscent of their baptism of fire, the men were once again in a vulnerable position on the federal right flank, exposed to fire from three sides. And, also somewhat eerily, the Connecticut soldiers were once again confronted by men of Stonewall Jackson's corps, under new command as a result of his death by friendly fire at Chancellorsville.

There is a debate among historians about Barlow's decision on where to position his troops, including the 17th: a few argue for urgent necessity, most others for foolhardy imprudence. In either case, these advancing units of XI Corps were essentially isolated and unprotected, asked to cover too much ground with too few resources.

Astride his handsome white horse, Lt. Colonel Douglas Fowler (replacing the absent Noble) led the

Francis Barlow: the ambitious "Boy General's" command decisions on July 1 at Gettysburg contributed to the costliest day of the war for Ridgefield.

companies of the Connecticut 17th forward to the knoll as enemy artillery roared, encouraging his men to "Dodge the big ones, boys". Moments later, a Confederate shell decapitated him.

By 3:45, the struggle was effectively over. Outnumbered and enveloped by a superior Rebel force, also as at Chancellorsville, the XI Corps retreated through the streets of Gettysburg. The 17th formed a defensive line south of town, initially at the foot of Cemetery Hill. The shattered remnants of the regiment successfully fought off Confederate attacks there and on higher ground, continuing to suffer casualties until Union victory was finally secured on July 3.

Of the 386 members of the regiment who were engaged, 206 were casualties, 96 by capture alone. And of the 23 Company G officers, sergeants, and corporals present before Chancellorsville, nearly half had been killed, wounded, or captured by Gettysburg's final day. For Ridgefield, July 1 had been the costliest day of the entire war by far, with 11 casualties.

One of the most tragic and poignant deaths was the village's own Sergeant Edwin Pickett.

From These Honored Dead

Eddie Pickett always stood out.

Perhaps it was because he was a son of "Boss" Pickett, a prominent Ridgefield citizen and operator and principal craftsman of a renowned cabinet-making firm, where young Eddie was learning the trade.

Or perhaps it was because this "taciturn country lad", as an acquaintance described him, demonstrated the attributes of a natural leader, as when he was the first to enlist following the August 9, 1862 town meeting, despite his marriage and position as a new father.

In any event, when several dozen Ridgefield men left for army service one week later, Eddie was one of only three individuals Anna Marie chose to identify by name in her journal. Once in the Connecticut 17th, he rose rapidly, and was promoted to sergeant by mid-November and to 1st sergeant a month before his death; as "Orderly" he was entrusted with running the company in the absence of its captain, and in

Their flags were a rallying point, a battlefield guide, a symbol of regimental honor—and a high-profile target.

preference to the lieutenants who were his nominal superiors.

As the men of the 17th advanced on Barlow's Knoll at Gettysburg on July 1, they were led by the flags that were the symbol of regimental honor—and a high-profile target. Years later, a comrade would recall: "Here Orderly Edwin D. Pickett was shot down while grasping the regimental colors, being the third bearer, who had carried them to the death."

The grave site of Eddie Pickett, who died a hero at Gettysburg.

Anna Marie's July 7, 1863 notations recording the federal victories at Gettysburg and Vicksburg with attendant bell-ringing and cannon-firing are followed by this poignant entry for July 12: *"The funeral of Eddie Pickett whose remains were brought home yesterday, is attended at our church this afternoon. A long procession of pedestrians, as well as carriages, followed his remains to the grave. His brother, Starr, searched some time among the dead at Gettysburg before he was found; his blanket was wrapped around him, his watch and pencil given by Starr were in his coat sleeve".*

The death of this promising young man evidently had a profound effect on the town. It is also emblematic of a significant change in the rituals surrounding death and burial.

Prior to the war, deaths usually occurred in the home, with most burials immediately thereafter, except when the frozen ground of winter made it impractical. Deaths on far-away battlefields were an unfamiliar phenomenon, and usually were treated in one of three ways: the bodies would be buried in shallow, often mass, graves near where they fell and ultimately re-interred elsewhere; fellow soldiers would contribute to the cost of preparation of the body and shipment home; or, as with Starr Pickett, a relative would retrieve the remains and return with them for burial.

In the latter two cases, the passage of time made preservation essential. Although embalming had been practiced before the war, its death toll vastly expanded the need and sped its routine adoption in civilian life. The 1850 census for Ridgefield, which lists several dozen occupations, has no mention of the trade; one Jacob Lockwood, a carpenter in 1860 and likely a builder of coffins, had expanded his services by 1870 and now declared himself to be an "Undertaker".

The looming presence of death on an unimaginable scale also pervaded the culture. One of the most common metaphors in song, art, and expression was the empty seat at the table or chair in the parlor, signifying the absent or forever departed loved one. Uncertainty added to the emotional and psychological pain; the fate of thousands of soldiers was simply unknown and, absent a breadwinner, families could become destitute.

Thanksgiving, which had long been marked in New England as a distinctly and wholly religious occasion, took on a civic and more secular connotation, as Lincoln proclaimed a national observation in 1863 and the government issued additional calls for days of thanksgiving or fasting thereafter.

The consequences of waging war bore down on the more quotidian aspects of life, as well, beginning with the disappearance of important southern markets for Ridgefield's furniture and carriage operations. There was also the matter of money.

As early as mid-1862, Anna Marie complained *"Specie has become so scarce that postage stamps of different values are substituted"*. Because the government required purchasers of the bonds it issued to finance the war to pay in specie—gold—which remained in Treasury vaults for weeks, money disappeared from circulation. To address the problem, the administration issued $150 million in Treasury Notes, or "greenbacks" not backed by gold reserves. At about the same time as Anna Marie's diary entry, a new Internal Revenue Act taxed almost everything, including income, introduced the concept of withholding, and, of course, established the Internal Revenue Bureau to administer it all.

While the combination of bond sales and tax increases mitigated the effects of wartime inflation, it did not eliminate them. By March 1863, Anna Marie commented that *"Many manufacture their own coffee out of burnt rye and wheat"* rather than pay 45 or 50 cents per pound. By spring, 1864, she observed that *"The high prices are alarming"* and later that *"Father goes to Norwalk, comes home discouraged"* by what he finds. Sugar had reached 26 cents a pound; good calico was 40 cents a yard; molasses was $1.10 per gallon. (It has been estimated that $1 in 1864 had the purchasing power of about $16.50 in 2008 money, while twenty-five cents was worth more than $4).

At the same time, the pressure for additional Union troops intensified. Ridgefield's enlistment bounty had been increased to $300 on July 1, 1863, while days later draft rioters in New York City focused their deadly wrath on African-Americans, including a children's orphanage.

In a turnabout, federal troops were dispatched from the Gettysburg battlefield to the city, where they joined local militia to suppress the violence.

About Used Up

In the aftermath of Gettysburg, the ill-starred XI Corps was broken up. General Howard and many of his soldiers were sent west, a tactic employed by both sides for exiling unsuccessful or difficult commanders. (Ironically, many historians agree that the Civil War was largely decided in the Western Theater.)

The 17th, now about used up, in the apt parlance of the time, and reduced to a few hundred men from the more than 1,000 who had left Bridgeport a year before, went south to the trenches on Morris Island in Charleston Harbor, where the opening shots of the war had been fired. There, in support of the August and September 1863 siege of Fort Wagner (an earlier unsuccessful assault forms the climax of the 1989 film "Glory"), the regiment battled disease, wielded shovels, and took cover from the constant Confederate shelling that frayed their nerves. In Colonel Noble's retrospective words, it "was about the most trying work the regiment ever did"—a remarkable judgment considering the 17th's devastating experiences between May and July.

Trial and Decision

As the conflict moved into its third year, the draft riots were only the most shocking evidence of war weariness. Enlistment bonuses ratcheted upwards (they would soar above $700 in Ridgefield by early 1865); wealthy men purchased substitutes for service; "bounty jumping" grew as an occupation; desertion rates increased to 200 per day. Although in the West the Mississippi now flowed "unvexed to the sea", in Lincoln's words, military affairs in the East were a litany of disappointment, the victory at Gettysburg notwithstanding. Citizens continued to purchase government bonds, to be sure, and communities continued to hold "soldiers' fairs" for the benefit of soldiers, sick men and hospitals at the front, as Anna Marie records that Ridgefield did in December 1863. But Gettysburg had come at an awful cost, and the public mood was not improved by new General Ulysses Grant's Overland Campaign of spring 1864, with its horrific 52,000 casualties in just over a month of fighting, followed by a months-long and deadly stalemate in the siege of Petersburg, Virginia.

Although anti-war "Copperheads", self-proclaimed in Ridgefield by the punched-out copper pennies they wore pinned to their hats, numbered only a handful in town, national and soldier sentiment regarding prosecution of the war was very much in question as the 1864 election loomed.

Opposing Abraham Lincoln was none other than George McClellan, whom the President had fired as commander of the Army of the Potomac in 1862, and who had defeated former Connecticut Governor Thomas Seymour, an avowed Copperhead, for the Democratic

Soldiers' Fairs, sometimes called Sanitary Fairs, were an opportunity for local communities to raise money and provide supplies for soldiers in the field and in hospitals.

nomination. Although he ultimately renounced much of his party's platform, McClellan was widely regarded as a "peace" candidate, appealing to those disaffected with the war. And there was the imponderable of the "soldier vote"; for the first time, some states permitted U.S. soldiers in the field to cast a presidential ballot. Would they support their beloved "Little Mac", who had turned them from farmhands and mechanics into an army, or vote for continued prosecution of a costly war under Lincoln?

The national mood was lifted, perhaps decisively, by General Sherman's capture of Atlanta in September 1864, prompting Anna Marie to declare with feeling *"The loyal North rejoices…"* and to predict Lincoln's re-election.

Once again, her intuition proved correct. Lincoln achieved nearly a 10 to 1 advantage in electoral votes while attracting 55 percent of the popular vote, and 70 percent of the "soldier vote". Connecticut, however, was a much nearer thing, and the "soldier vote" was decisive. Lincoln's statewide popular advantage was a mere 2,406 votes; Connecticut troops provided him with a margin of 2,898. The President carried Ridgefield by 79 votes, compared with an advantage of 144 four years earlier.

Florida Sojourn

By February 1864 what remained of the original Connecticut 17th was on the move again, this time to a relative backwater in the piney woods of northeast Florida, first to Jacksonville and then to St. Augustine. As they marched and counter-marched through the next year, often to little purpose, and left their outposts along the St. John's River for brief expeditions into the Confederate interior, the men battled heat, disease, insects, and boredom, interrupted by the occasional unpleasant surprise at the hands of Confederate guerillas.

For example, Colonel Noble himself was captured on Christmas Eve 1864 and sent to the notorious Confederate prison at Andersonville, Georgia, where he became the highest-ranking Union officer confined to the place. Not long after, he was freed while attempting to tunnel his way to escape.

Then, in February 1865, a federal raiding party returning from the capture of cotton at Braddock's Farm (also called Dunn's Lake) ended with a Rebel ambush, the death of the commanding officer, and the capture of two captains and at least 30 men, including Ridgefield's unlucky John Jarvis, who had survived earlier capture at Gettysburg only to find himself a prisoner once again. The men who were taken joined Colonel Noble at Andersonville. He can be forgiven for amending his earlier judgment and deciding years later that "the mass of the regiment never had harder or more taxing service than in Florida".

Victory and Mourning

Grant's strategy of attrition—of using the southern defense of Richmond as the stone on which to grind Lee's army to pieces—was costly but successful, and the Confederate commander surrendered his Army of Northern Virginia on April 9, 1865, effectively ending the war almost four years to the day after it had begun. Anna Marie greeted the announcement this way: *"News which causes devout Thanksgiving to ascend from thousands of hearts comes to us, the surrender of Lee's army."*

The day before, President Abraham Lincoln had visited wounded federal soldiers at City Point, Virginia. Before a delighted crowd, and in top hat and long black frock coat, Lincoln picked up an axe and began chopping wood. Soldiers grabbed the chips as souvenirs. One of them was Jacob Legrand Dauchy of Ridgefield, a musician in the 11th Connecticut, who regaled listeners for years with his tale of "The Railsplitter's" last use of an axe.

Only days later came this entry in Anna Marie's journal: *"The Tribune comes clad in mourning announcing the awful intelligence that our President Abraham Lincoln was assassinated..."* At noon on April 19, the same hour as the slain president's funeral in Washington, D. C., all churches in Ridgefield were filled with mourners attending special services; businesses were closed for the day.

As with events at Bull Run almost four years before, the feeling of deep anguish was not universally shared. Informed of the news of Lincoln's assassination, an unsympathetic (and prominent) Ridgefield resident declared: "He wasn't shot a minute too quick!"

The last months of the war had passed uneventfully for the Connecticut 17th, and the regiment was mustered out of service on July 19, 1865 at Hilton Head, South Carolina. If there was a victory parade or community celebration for Ridgefield soldiers when they returned home, it has gone unrecorded.

Epilogue

The Civil War cast a long political shadow. Seven Union veterans served as president, William McKinley being the last; another eight Union generals ran for the office. The association of former Union soldiers, the Grand Army of the Republic (GAR), was a powerful force lobbying for their interests up to the turn of the 20th century.

Decoration Day, when the graves of fallen Civil War soldiers were marked, was first commemorated in 1868 and now honors all veterans as Memorial Day. There is a monument to the 17th Connecticut on Barlow's Knoll at Gettysburg, as well as a 1924 memorial to Ridgefield service members including Civil War soldiers on Main Street in front of the Jesse Lee United Methodist Church. While accounts vary, it is likely that Ridgefield suffered at least 6 men killed as a result of combat, while some 16 perished from disease, imprisonment, or misadventure. Approximately twenty-seven were wounded during the course of the war, 26 were captured, and 18 soldiers deserted.

Hiram (right), one of three long-lived Davis brothers, was the last Civil War veteran to have lived in Ridgefield when he died in 1947.

Eddie Pickett, for whom Ridgefield GAR Post 64 was named, is buried in Titicus Cemetery[3] as is the largest number of local Civil War veterans; another group rests in the Branchville Cemetery.

On August 28, 1884, weeks after the dedication of the Gettysburg monument, a Ridgefield reunion was held to commemorate the mustering-in of the 17th Connecticut. Twenty-one local men were among the 400 who attended. They were greeted by 2,000 townspeople as they marched through village streets, met at city hall, and gathered for a picnic on the Lounsbury grounds, now Veterans' Park.

Membership in GAR Post 64 dwindled until the few remaining survivors were absorbed by the Danbury unit around 1900.

Anna Marie Resseguie died in March 1913 at the age of 82. She had no descendants.

A late-war enlistee in the 25th New York Cavalry—a 15-year-old drummer boy named Hiram Davis—was the last Civil War veteran to spend most of his life in Ridgefield and one of the last in Connecticut and the country when he passed away at age 98 in 1947.

Notes

[1] Assembled in one place, or even two or three, the approximately 100 shoemakers would have been a considerable commercial presence, almost certainly the largest in Ridgefield. If such a sizeable operation existed, it has gone unrecorded.

A likelier possibility is that shoemaking was actually a cottage industry practiced in individual homes to supplement farming or other occupations, with different men (and women) specializing in various steps of the shoemaking process. Such "putting out" was a common practice in the New England of the period. For example, the March 26, 1860 issue of the New York Times reported that "The Ridgefield Shirt Factory employs 1,100 women who sew shirts in their homes." This activity must have included many ladies in neighboring towns, since such a workforce would have required participation by every female in Ridgefield, from newborn to nonagenarian. Whether it was shoemaking or shirtmaking, however, substantial capital as well as an extensive and very active carting network or busy central depot would have been required to provide tools, deliver raw materials, transport partially-completed items, and collect and ship finished goods. There is no record in the 1850 census of anyone engaged in such an occupation, unless one of a number of men listed simply as "Merchant", possibly one or more tannery owners, was also operating a contract shoemaking business, while some of the many individuals listed as "Laborer" were actually teamsters.

[2] Corporal Henry Keeler is an illustration of the "fog of war" or—perhaps more specifically—the fog that can shroud lives and record-keeping from 150 years ago.

Official state and regimental records have Corporal Keeler enlisting in the 14th Connecticut Volunteer Infantry on August 2, 1862 as a "resident" of Waterbury. Blaikie Hines' rigorous compilation of Civil War service statistics for individual Connecticut communities, which largely relies on the same sources, does not include him in its Ridgefield chapter. What is more, Corporal Keeler's name is conspicuously missing from the several Keeler men in the list of Civil War veterans on Ridgefield's 1924 Main Street monument. Considering that the particulars of his life and death would have been present in the memories of village citizens, especially among the large number of his Keeler relatives in town, the omission is unlikely to have been an accident.

And yet, in his 1927 town history (and almost as a challenge to the decision of the monument committee), George Rockwell lists Corporal Keeler, mortally wounded September 17, 1862 at the Battle of Antietam after just six weeks of duty, among Ridgefield men who served in the Civil War, with the notation that he "enlisted from Waterbury". Subsequent writers have identified Keeler as Ridgefield's first battlefield fatality.

Supporting Rockwell's attribution, Anna Marie Resseguie's November 2, 1862 journal entry—discovered decades after Rockwell wrote—clearly describes the recovery of Keeler's body from the battlefield by his Ridgefield brother (anticipating Eddie Pickett's repatriation 10 months later), his Ridgefield church membership, and his Ridgefield funeral and burial. Anna Marie is, however, somewhat vague about the particulars of Keeler's Ridgefield residency.

So: which community's claim is more convincing? This writer is persuaded that the answer can be found in the very different replies to the questions "Where do you live?" and "What town are you from?"

Corporal Keeler was undoubtedly a Ridgefield native, with strong local ties, and we may never know what led him to be in Waterbury, or for how long. Employment in that city's booming brass factories? "Bounty shopping"? Personal reasons?

There must have been a compelling motive for Keeler's decision to join up in Waterbury on August 2, 1862, when his Ridgefield relatives, friends and neighbors were enlisting in his hometown and he could have joined them in a "local" regiment and company. And to explain why Keeler enlisted in Waterbury a scant seven days before Ridgefield offered a $200 recruitment bonus—something likely to have been rumored in advance.

As with many individual decisions and motivations from so long ago, the answers are likely to remain unknown—and unknowable. For the purposes of this history, the circumstances of Keeler's retrieval and burial, Rockwell's attribution, and the subsequent discovery of Anna Marie's confirming journal entry are conclusive: he is considered Ridgefield's first battlefield death of the Civil War.

[3]Among the valiant soldiers who rest in Ridgefield's cemeteries, Edwin Pickett stands in the front rank, literally as well as metaphorically. His weathered headstone—twice broken and repaired—is unique; the carving of a hand grasping a flag at its top commemorates the brave circumstances of Pickett's death. Appropriately and somewhat symbolically, his grave has a line of sight to the Ridgefield American Legion hall on North Salem Road.

Edward Knox (1841?-1916) was a larger-than-life Ridgefield resident who also achieved distinction for his Civil War service. He was a second lieutenant with the 15th New York Light Artillary, part of the famed Irish Brigade, and a veteran of the Battles of Fredricksburg and Chancellorsville when he participated in the desperate July 2 fighting near the Peach Orchard at Gettysburg. After the war, Knox took over and turned around the family's floundering hat business. A successful and wealthy businessman, he built a mansion of some 50 rooms on a huge parcel on the north side of Florida Hill Road, where Mark Twain was a frequent visitor. Knox also built a far more modest dwelling for neighbor George Washington Gilbert, the "Hermit of Ridgefield".

In 1892, Congress voted Knox the Medal of Honor for his bravery at Gettysburg, one of 83 men so honored, and one of more than 1,500 who received the award during the Civil War, compared with 464 in World War II, after the criteria were made much more restrictive. Knox was cited for holding his ground until compelled to draw his artillery piece off by hand; he was severely wounded. A second version has the quick-witted Knox ordering his men to "play dead" at their guns as Confederates overran their position. Following a successful Union counter-attack, the men sprang to their feet and withdrew their cannon to safety.

It is at least possible that Knox received his award nearly 30 years after the fact in part because of his post-war business and social prominence. The Grand Army of the Republic presented him with a jeweled sword of honor as "the most popular and handsomest officer of the encampment" and he was later elected colonel of the 69th Regiment, a title he used for the rest of his life.

Principal Sources

1850, 1860, 1870 Census Records for Ridgefield, Connecticut

Battle Cry of Freedom, James McPherson, 1988.

Civil War—Volunteer Sons of Connecticut, Blaikie Hines, 2002.

The Civil War Book of Lists, Combined Books, 1994.

History of Fairfield County, William H. Noble, 1881.

History of Ridgefield, George Rockwell, 1927.

Record of Service of Connecticut Men in the Army and Navy of the United States During the War of the Rebellion, 1889.

RidgefieldHistory.com, Jack Sanders, Webmaster.

Ridgefield in Review, Silvio Bedini, 1958.

A View From The Inn: The Journal of Anna Marie Resseguie. Keeler Tavern Preservation Society, 1993.

17thcvi.org, Dale E. Call, Webmaster.

Illustration Credits

Page 2—Keeler Tavern Museum

Page 4—Keeler Tavern Museum

Page 8—Keeler Tavern Museum

Page 12—Ridgefield Historical Society

Page 17—U.S. Military History Institute

Page 33—Smithsonian Gallery

Page 37--Ridgefield Historical Society

Appendix

Learning More About Your Ridgefield Civil War Ancestor

Here are some helpful resources for learning more about your Ridgefield Civil War ancestor:

Record of Service of Connecticut Men in the Army and Navy of the United States During the War of the Rebellion, 1889. The most comprehensive and reliable index of the men who served, when and where they enrolled, their rank(s), unit(s), and disposition. A copy is available at the Ridgefield Historical Society in the Scott House.

cyndislist.com Information on how to obtain your veteran ancestor's pension records from the National Archives.

History of Ridgefield by George Rockwell. The chapter on the Civil War contains the author's list of Ridgefielders who served in the war, together with notations on dates, units, etc. Also contains extensive information on prominent local families. Copies are available at the Ridgefield Library and the Historical Society, as well as for purchase online at digital-editions.com/RIDGEFIELD.

Ridgefield Memorial. Located on Main Street in front of Jesse Lee United Methodist Church, across from the Route 102 intersection. The north face lists one accounting of Ridgefield Civil War veterans.

17cvi.org. This website contains extensive information—including the roster—for the 17th Connecticut Volunteer

Infantry regiment, much of it drawn from offricial records. More than 60 Ridgefield men—more than one-quarter of the war's total—served in companies C and G.

The greatest number of Ridgefield Civil War veterans is buried in the Ridgefield Cemetery (bounded by North Street, North Salem Road [Route 116], and Mapleshade Road), and in Branchville Cemetery (near the intersection of Routes 102 and 7). Here are some suggestions to start your search:

For an orientation to Ridgefield's cemeteries, consult RidgefieldHistory.com and click on "Cemeteries" for general maps and information, as well as for instructions on making limited e-mail inquiries about specific individuals.

To locate the cemetery in which your ancestor may be buried, visit the Ridgefield Historical Society to consult the 1934 WPA-produced index to individual burial plots, or their other related resources. Arrangements also available through RidgefieldHistory.com.

About the Author

Charles Pankenier has studied the Civil War for more than 50 years, and has visited sites of Civil War conflict from St. Albans, Vermont to Honey Springs, Oklahoma, many of them as part of Smithsonian study groups. He has walked more than 40 battlefields in the footsteps of Civil War soldiers from both North and South, and has come away with a single over-riding question: "How did they summon the courage?"

The author continues to pursue his interest in history as a member of Connecticut's Fairfield County Civil War Roundtable and as a guide at Ridgefield's historic Keeler Tavern Museum.

保

This is a Worthy Shorts keepsake. It is designed to preserve words and images of value to its author. We honor its intent with the Chinese character for "preserve," a word picture created more than 3,000 years ago.

This book is typeset in Berkeley